DID YOU KNOW?

The hottest temperature of 134°F (57°C) was recorded in North America on July 10, 1913, at Furnace Creek, Death Valley, California.

The current depth record by free scuba diving is an incredible 1,083 feet (330 meters), which is approximately the height of a 100-story skyscraper.

Mount Thor on Baffin Island in the Canadian Arctic is thought to be the highest purely vertical fall at 4,100 feet (1,250 meters).

Fresh lava ranges from 1,300°F to 2,200°F (700°C to 1,200°C) and glows red to white hot as it flows.

Imagine yourself exploring the most extreme parts of our amazing planet—trekking though the driest desert, climbing the snowiest mountaintops, and diving to the deepest regions of the ocean floor. Join Seymour Simon as he transports you to extreme destinations, introducing you to Earth's biggest, smallest, deepest, and coldest environments, animals, plants, and weather! These mind-bending facts and stunning photographs invite you on an exciting, and sometimes unbelievable, scientific expedition of Earth's most amazing records!

Praise for *Seymour Simon's Extreme Earth Records*:

"Simon knows how to attract young fact mongers."
    —*School Library Journal*

"An artful blend of text and image."
    —*Kirkus Reviews*

"This is a title that will never stay on the shelf."
    —*Library Media Connection*

"A lively trip."
    —*SLJ Teen*

SEYMOUR SIMON'S EXTREME EARTH RECORDS

By Seymour Simon

chronicle books · san francisco

To Liz Nealon with love. My companion, collaborator, and wife who helped create this book. —S.S.

First Chronicle Books LLC paperback edition, published in 2015.
Originally published in hardcover in 2012 by Chronicle Books LLC.

Text copyright © 2012 by Seymour Simon.

ISBN 978-1-4521-2879-5

The Library of Congress has cataloged the original edition as follows:

Simon, Seymour.
Seymour Simon's extreme earth records / by Seymour Simon.
p. cm.
ISBN 978-1-4521-0785-1 (alk. paper)
1. Earth—Juvenile literature. I. Title. II. Title: Extreme earth records.
QB631.4.S535 2012
550—dc23

2011045937

Manufactured in China.

Book design by Amelia May Mack.
Typeset in Bryant and Yumi.

10 9 8 7 6 5 4 3 2 1

Chronicle Books LLC
680 Second Street
San Francisco, California 94107

Chronicle Books—we see things differently.
Become part of our community at www.chroniclekids.c

Table of Contents

The Coldest Place on Earth

When you step off the plane onto the rocky ice, you will immediately struggle with challenges that will last anywhere from one to eight weeks, as you acclimate yourself to the coldest place on Earth, Vostok Research Station in Antarctica.

During this time you suffer from pounding headaches, painful earaches, and constant nosebleeds. Your eyes twitch and you vomit—a lot. You find yourself short of breath and feel as if you're suffocating due to the lack of oxygen. You can't sleep because of all your discomforts. Your blood pressure rises and you have painful cramps in your arms and legs. Sounds like a perfect vacation from school, doesn't it?

Vostok Station is a lonely, windblown outpost 621 miles (1,000 kilometers) from the South Pole. It holds the record for the lowest recorded temperature on Earth, -128.6°F (-89.2°C), recorded in July 1983. Twice a year, tractor-train (a train of tractor trucks) expeditions take as long as a month to crawl dangerously over the cracked, icy landscape, carrying food and supplies to about a dozen Russian, American, and French scientists who live there conducting a variety of experiments.

Scientists are drilling down through thick layers of ice beneath Vostok Research Station, the coldest place on Earth. The spinning drills have reached down to gigantic Lake Vostok, which lies more than 2 miles (3.2 kilometers) deep inside the icy glacier. The core of ice removed from the drilling dates back to more than 420,000 years ago, a time when saber-toothed tigers and woolly mammoths roamed the earth. The drilling stops just short of the waters in the lake. Scientists are trying to keep the unseen lake waters pure and uncontaminated by bacteria the drills carry from the surface. Scientists study the tubes of ice to learn more about the kinds of microbial life that may have existed in the waters, despite the high pressure, constant cold, and lack of sunlight. What kinds of life can live in

Vostok

How cold is cold?

Water freezes at 32° F (0°C). Ice cream needs to be stored at approximately -10° F (-23°C) to remain solid. At -50° F (-45°C), you can get frostbite on your unprotected fingers or nose within a few minutes. The coldest temperature ever recorded in the United States was -80° F (-62°C), in Alaska.

the cold lake waters inside an icy glacier is a scientific mystery that remains to be solved.

Of course, it is not always *that* cold in Vostok, but it is always *very* cold. The high temperature even in the "warmer months" of the Antarctic summer is often a bone-chilling -60°F (-51°C). There is no sign of animal life outside the station, except for the occasional skua bird—it's too cold for living things in the "South Pole of Cold."

The Jupiter and Saturn Connection

Antarctica was once warm enough for many kinds of plants and animals to live. But not today, and not down deep inside a glacier. Since Antarctica froze over, Lake Vostok has been completely sealed from outside air and sunlight. Not a single ray of light has reached the cold waters in hundreds of thousands of years. Yet scientists think that some kinds of life can live even in such a dark place. If any life is able to survive in Lake Vostok, it may be similar to the life that might exist in the ice-covered oceans on one of Jupiter's moons, Europa, and one of Saturn's moons, Enceladus. We won't know for sure unless spacecraft or robots from Earth touch down on Europa or Enceladus to search their hidden oceans for life. But the clues to the life on distant moons may lie in a frozen lake in Antarctica.

The Hottest Place on Earth

Imagine yourself on a hot, sandy beach on a beautiful summer day. Your feet feel like they are on fire and you want to run and dip them in the cool ocean water. The temperature on the beach reaches more than 100°F (38°C). That is hot—very hot. But 134°F (57°C) is even hotter!

The record-breaking highest temperature in North America of 134°F (57°C) was recorded on July 10, 1913, at Furnace Creek in Death Valley, California.

The creek is well named because it feels like a furnace in the summer. The population of the village of Furnace Creek is only twenty-four people, according to the latest census. Why? Probably because no one wants to live in that heat!

Ordinary summer heat is bad in the desert lands of the Southwest United States, but in Death Valley it really sizzles from June through August. Winds from surrounding mountain ranges blow hot, dry air thousands of feet down into the long, narrow valley called Death. Death Valley's lowest point is 282 feet (86 meters) below sea level. As air moves downhill, it heats up and becomes 5.5°F hotter for every drop of 1,000 feet (or 10°C per kilometer drop). And because of the high elevation of the nearby Sierra Nevada mountain range, the air is warmed 20°F to 30°F (11°C to 17°C) by the time it reaches the valley floor, making the already hot air feel like the inside of an oven.

Yet even in that heat, Death Valley is home to a variety of plants, birds, fish, and reptiles that have adapted to the heat. Coyotes, ravens, roadrunners, antelope squirrels, black-tailed jack rabbits, snakes, and lizards have all found ways to survive the high temperatures. Some come out only in the early morning or late afternoon, when the sun is not high in the sky and it's not as hot. Bighorn sheep roam the mountains around Death Valley. And some dangerous animals live here, including rattlesnakes, scorpions, black widow spiders, bees, and wasps.

You too can visit Death Valley in the summer, but only if you are prepared and use common sense. You can safely tour in an air-conditioned vehicle, sticking to paved roads. Always bring plenty of water in case of emergency, and drink often—at least one or two gallons per day. Summer hiking is not recommended.

Why is it called Death Valley?

Death Valley was given its deadly name by a group of pioneers lost there in the winter of 1849–1850. They thought that they would die there. But the pioneers were rescued by two young men from their group, who scouted a way out. Legend has it that as the wagon train pulled over the mountains around the valley, one of the party looked back and said, "Good-bye, Death Valley." The name and the story of the Lost '49ers have become part of the history of the United States West.

Even hotter temperatures than those recorded in scorching days in Death Valley have been measured in the Lut Desert in Iran. The Lut is a salt desert, partly covered with salt flats and volcanic lava. The black volcanic rock absorbs heat, while much of the rest of the desert is a sea of sand. The giant sand dunes are more than 1,000 feet (305 meters) high—taller than the Eiffel Tower! A NASA satellite measured temperatures as high as 160°F (71°C), the hottest surface temperature ever recorded on Earth. Few living things can survive for long at these blistering temperatures. In fact, the pasteurized milk you drink every day is usually heated to 161°F (72°C) to kill harmful bacteria, yeast, and mold. It seems as if the Lut Desert might be the most bacteria-free place on Earth!

How hot is hot?

Most people feel comfortable when the air temperature is between 68°F and 80°F (20°C and 27°C). Your body temperature is 98.6°F (37°C). Constant temperatures above 105°F (40°C) can overwhelm the body and lead to serious and even fatal heatstroke and loss of consciousness. No human being could survive for more than a few minutes in the hottest places in Death Valley.

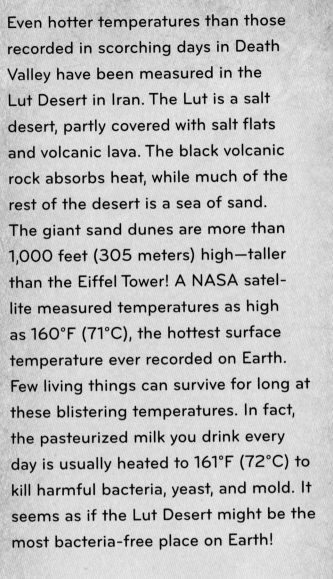

IRAN

The Most Remote Place on Earth

Do you ever feel like you want to get away from everything—school, siblings, and parents? Then Tristan da Cunha is the place to go! Tristan da Cunha is the most remote place in the world—no one will be able to find you, probably because it is so difficult to get here.

Tristan da Cunha rises out of the middle of the sea like a creature from the ocean's depths. It is a rocky volcanic peak about the size of a small city, with only about 2 square miles (5 square kilometers) of flat area, where the islanders grow potatoes. Narrow ravines leading down from the central peak become torrents of fast-running water during the rainy season, making it hard to get around an island that is already hard to get to. The steep, rocky coastline is often battered by storm-tossed waters. Tristan da Cunha is one in a small group of five islands in the South Atlantic Ocean. It has a population of approximately 300 people, who share the islands with a dozen species of seabirds, including the rockhopper penguin and several kinds of albatross. It would take about a week to get to Tristan from South Africa, the nearest mainland port. The closest land masses are South Africa, at 1,750 miles (2,816 kilometers) to the east, and South America, 2,088 miles (3,360 kilometers) to the west.

Most of the year, clouds shroud the snow-topped volcanic peak on the island. In 1961, a volcano erupted on the island of Tristan. All of the inhabitants were taken 20 miles (32 kilometers) to Nightingale

Island, a tiny uninhabited island nearby. Many people left to live in England, but almost all moved back in 1963 when the volcano stopped erupting and it was safe to return.

Today, Tristan has a school, hospital, post office, museum, and crayfish-canning factory. The post office issues stamps that are collected around the world. The people on the island support themselves by fishing, raising livestock, growing simple crops, and making handicrafts. There is no airport or landing field on the island, but Tristan is visited by fishing boats and a ship that brings supplies once a year. The residents can order things online, but there is no overnight delivery. It could take up to a year to get your package—that is what happens when you live in the most remote place in the world. In case you're ever on Tristan and want to order online, the island has a United Kingdom postal code that is TDCU 1ZZ.

What's hopping?

The rockhopper penguins that live on Tristan's rocky shores are part of a family of crested penguins with brightly colored feathers on their heads. Their yellow feathers look like long eyebrows. They get their name because they hop over the rocks on the shores where they live. Rockhopper penguins are loud, noisy, and aggressive birds. They will quickly attack anyone or anything that bothers them. They make a nest by scraping a hole in the ground and lining it with dead grass. Two eggs are typically laid in the nest. Usually the second egg is larger, and the chick that hatches from that egg has a better chance of survival.

What do you find in the capital of the loneliest place on Earth?

The capital of the island is named Edinburgh of the Seven Seas, in honor of a visit by Queen Victoria's son, Prince Alfred, Duke of Edinburgh, in 1867. The small town is home to a village hall, a museum, a post office, a café, a shop, a school, fisheries, and a few churches.

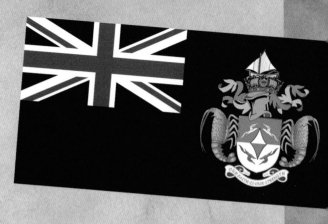

The Deepest Place on Earth

If you dove deep into the water from a boat, you might get down to about 10 feet (3 meters). The pressure of the air in your lungs and the limits of how long you could hold your breath would soon force you to the surface. But the ocean is much, much deeper than that.

If Mount Everest, the tallest mountain in the world, were dropped into the deepest part of the ocean, it would still be covered by more than a mile (1.6 kilometers) of water! The deepest place on Earth is the Challenger Deep in the Mariana Trench in the Pacific Ocean. The Challenger Deep is approximately 7 miles (11 kilometers) below sea level. That is much deeper than the ocean near the shore. The sun cannot penetrate the ocean at the depth of the Challenger Deep, making the water very dark and cold. The pressure is enormous—16,000 pounds (7,257 kilograms) per square inch. That much pressure would feel as if there were one elephant standing atop every little postage stamp–sized spot on your body. Left unprotected, you would be crushed!

The only people ever to explore the Challenger Deep were Swiss scientist Jacques Piccard and United States Navy officer Donald Walsh, in January 1960. They descended to the bottom of the world in the Trieste, a heavily armored, deep-diving submersible called a bathyscaphe. The Trieste bathyscaphe took four hours and forty-eight minutes descending at 3 feet (1 meter) per second to get to the floor of the Challenger Deep.

On the way down, one of the outer Plexiglas windowpanes cracked, shaking the entire vessel. While on the floor of the Deep, Piccard and Walsh used a sonar phone to keep in contact with the surface ship. At a speed of approximately 1 mile (1.6 kilometers) per second (about five times the speed of sound in air), it took seven seconds for a voice message to travel from the Trieste to the surface ship, and another seven seconds for answers to return. No other humans have ever reached as deep down as Piccard and Walsh descended in 1960. The two observed many kinds of fish, crabs, shrimp, and other creatures living on

Depth in meters

0

2,000

4,000

6,000

8,000

10,000

11,035

Mt. Everest (8,848 meters above sea level)

Mariana Trench

11,035 meters below sea level

Get in the zone!

The ocean can be divided into five zones depending on the amount of sunlight received. The top layer, the sunlit zone, goes down from the surface to approximately 590 feet (180 meters). Most fish, dolphins, and other sea mammals and plankton live in this zone. The middle zone, the twilight zone, begins where the sunlit zone ends and goes down to 2,950 feet (900 meters). Many kinds of fish, jellyfish, and squid live in the twilight zone. About 90 percent of the ocean is in the next zone, the midnight zone, and below. The deepest zones of the ocean are called the abyss and, below it, the hadal zone. It is entirely dark so far down, with no light from the surface. The water pressure is extreme. The temperature is near freezing. Yet anglerfish, sea cucumbers, snipe eels, opossum shrimp, vampire squid, and hordes of bacteria live in these dark, cold, pressurized waters.

How far down can people dive in scuba gear?

The current depth record by free scuba (self-contained underwater breathing apparatus) diving is an incredible 1,083 feet (330 meters), about the height of a 100-story skyscraper. But that's much deeper than would be safe for most scuba divers. The maximum recommended depth for a certified, experienced scuba diver breathing compressed air is 130 feet (40 meters). Any greater depth is very risky. The deeper a diver descends, the shorter the time the diver can remain underwater. Divers going 130 feet (40 meters) down can stay only ten minutes before they need to go through a series of decompression stops every few feet to the surface to avoid getting the "bends," nitrogen bubbles in their blood that might cause injury and even death.

the seafloor. One oddity they saw is a deep-sea anglerfish that uses a bioluminescent "life light" as a lure to attract prey.

The bottom of the Challenger Deep is covered by hydrothermal vents—geysers on the seafloor. The vents gush superhot, mineral-rich water that can reach 570°F (300°C). Boiling water in a teapot is only 212°F (100°C)! You would think that no animal could survive those temperatures. Yet whole communities of living things, from bacteria and worms to clusters of ghostly white vent crabs, live near these hot pulses of water.

The Highest Place on Earth

Mount Everest in Nepal's Himalaya Mountains is the tallest mountain on Earth, almost 5½ miles (29,029 feet or 8,848 meters) above sea level. That's approximately 6,000 times as tall as you are.

Because of upward pressures within the earth, Everest is probably getting a few inches taller every year—this means that just like you, the highest point on Earth keeps growing! Mount Everest is as tall as twenty Empire State Buildings stacked one on top of another. More than 4,000 people have tried to climb the mountain, but far fewer have actually reached the summit. Mount Everest is dangerous; nearly 200 people have died on the slopes of the mountain. Most who reach the top stay a few minutes and then just climb back down. But at least one person skied part of the way down, and another person came down from the peak in just eleven minutes by paragliding.

Hurricane-strength winds blast the rocky, icy peaks of Everest most of the year. The winds are part of the jet stream, a band of rapidly moving winds that blow approximately 4 to 6 miles (6 to 10 kilometers) above Earth's surface. A tail of ice crystals floats off the top of the mountain when the jet stream is blowing. If you want to climb to the summit of Everest, you have to choose the time carefully. There is a small window in the spring and another in the fall when the jet stream is not blowing directly across the famous mountaintop.

Everest was first climbed in 1953 by Tenzing Norgay, of Nepal, and Edmund Hillary, of New Zealand. Climbers need to prepare their bodies for the harsh conditions on Everest. The air is very thin atop the mountain. There is approximately one third of the oxygen at the peak than there is at sea level. This makes it difficult to breathe and accomplish the smallest of tasks, like walking or setting up camp. Climbers establish a camp at the base of the mountain and four successively higher camps before trying to reach the summit. They rest one day for every 1,000 feet (305 meters) they may climb the previous day.

Is there life on Mount Everest?

The lower parts of Mount Everest are forested with stands of birch, fir, and pine trees. As the altitude increases, only dwarf trees or shrubs grow. Still higher, you find only lichens and mosses. Plants can't develop in snow, so they disappear at the permanent snow line above 18,500 feet (5,639 meters). Animals that live up high have furry coats that help them retain body heat. Himalayan bears find sheltered caves in which they hibernate in winter months, when food is not easily available. Yaks are used as beasts of burden by the sherpas on Mount Everest.

The scariest aluminum ladders in the world?

The Khumbu Icefall is the most dangerous part of the climb to the top of Mount Everest. The icefall is a fantastic jumble of constantly shifting huge blocks of ice called seracs. The seracs slide against each other, pieces break off, and new deep cracks open up; all of this means it is very treacherous going. Walking or hiking with metal spikes on your shoes across the Khumbu means burying pickets in the ice, fixing rope lines from one picket to another, clipping and unclipping from one rope to another as you go, and crossing deep, scary cracks on aluminum ladders. For larger cracks in the ice, two or three ladders can be tied together, making a longer but more unstable platform. More climbers have died in the Khumbu Icefall than on any other part of the mountain.

Besides the lack of oxygen and the winds that climbers face, Everest is also very cold. Temperatures on the high peaks often drop to -100°F (-73°C). Even on a nice summer day, temperatures at base camp at night may be well below freezing. The climb is also very difficult because men and women lose their footing on the unstable snow and ice. Climbers often use aluminum ladders to go up and down the icy mountain's sides.

The Rainiest Place on Earth

Imagine rain falling steadily every day for a week. You can't go outside and play, your shoes and pants are constantly wet, and there are puddles on every street corner. Now imagine rain falling nearly every day for an entire year!

That is what it is like in the wettest place on Earth. Mount Waialeale on the island of Kauai in the Hawaiian Islands averages more than 450 inches (1,143 centimeters) of rain a year! And the record of 683 inches (1,735 centimeters) a year was set in 1982. That's about the height of a six-story building.

Waialeale means "overflowing water" in Hawaiian, and that is what it is like on the mountain. The huge amount of rain produces a large, marshy bog around the mountain that makes walking difficult—pants would be wet and shoes would be full of mud here! The area is part of a wilderness preserve that is home to many rare plants. One of the rarest plants is a kind of geranium known as the Kauai geranium, or called by its Hawaiian name, *hinahina*. It's a small shrub with a few purple-striped white flowers. The Kauai geranium was put on the United States' list of endangered plant species in 2010. There are fewer than 200 of these plants left in the entire world.

The two wettest weather stations in the United States are in Yakutat, Alaska, with an average of 160 inches (406 centimeters) of precipitation and 235 wet days a year, and Hilo, Hawaii, with 126 inches (320 centimeters) of rain and 278 rainy days a year. In the rest of the country, the most rain- and snowfall have been measured on Mount Washington, in New Hampshire, and Quillayute, Washington. These two weather stations sit thousands of miles apart from each other on opposite sides of the United States. But they both get approximately 102 inches (259 centimeters) of precipitation a year and are nearly tied for the total days per year it rains or snows (209 compared to 208 days). The rainiest U.S. cities, such as West Palm Beach and New Orleans, are mostly in Florida and Louisiana. But Mobile, Alabama, and Port Arthur, Texas, are also in the list of the top ten rainiest U.S. cities.

Other rainiest places on Earth:

- Lloró, Columbia, gets an average of 40 feet or 480 inches (1,220 centimeters) of rain a year. It rains nearly every day of the year, rivaling Waialeale as the world-record holder.

- Cherrapunji and Mawsynram, in northeast India, also get a large amount of rain, but unlike Mount Waialeale and Lloró, most of the rain in India falls between June and August. This is known as the monsoon, or the wet season. Although Cherrapunji is slightly less rainy on average than Mount Waialeale and Lloró, it holds the single-year record of 1,042 inches (2,647 centimeters), measured in 1861.

- Milford Sound in New Zealand gets an average of 266 inches (676 centimeters) of rain every year. It rains an average of 180 days every year—about every other day.

Even the best umbrella and raincoat are not much of a defense against the large amount of rain that falls in these places.

What is a monsoon?

In the tropics, the wet or rainy season is a particular time of year that lasts for a month or longer. When rainfall comes with a wind shift (a change in direction of the wind at 45 degrees or more for a period of 15 minutes), the wet season is called a monsoon. Tropical rain forests don't have wet seasons, because their rainfall occurs throughout the year. In places with a wet or rainy season, the rain usually falls heavily in the late afternoon and early evening. Plants grow in large numbers and can get to be huge in size, rivers often overflow, and some animals

The Driest Place on Earth

The Atacama Desert in northern Chile is the driest desert in the world. Some parts of the desert have not seen rain for centuries. Most of Earth is covered by oceans, but approximately one-third is dry land. And one-third of that dry land is called desert, really dry land.

Most of the world's deserts are found in the subtropical zones north of the Tropic of Cancer and south of the Tropic of Capricorn. There is very little rainfall in these deserts—less than 10 inches (25 centimeters) a year—and they can't support much plant or animal life. How long do you think you could survive without water? In temperatures above 90°F (32°C), no one could live without water for more than four or five days. Plants in a hot desert are usually cacti and other ground-hugging shrubs and small woody trees. Water is stored in the roots, stems, and leaves of the plants. These fleshy plants are called succulents. Many desert plants, such as the prickly pear cactus, can lose water out from their leaves and dry up but still remain alive. Cacti survive because they have a thick waxy coating on the outside of their stems and leaves. This helps them retain water and protects them from intense sunlight. Other desert plants have leaves that are shiny, which reflects the sun, or leaves that that stand up and down, which minimizes the surface area directly hit by light. While some parts of the Atacama along the coast have plants such as cacti, the drier parts of the desert have no plants at all. These arid regions don't even have the microscopic green plants that live in rocks or under stones in most other deserts.

Birds and mammals need a certain amount of water to survive. Desert animals have an efficient kind of water-balancing budget or system to balance water income and water expense. Water income comes from liquid drunk, water in foods, or the water produced in a body when food is digested. Water expense is caused by evaporation, excretion of urine and feces, and egg or milk production. A 10 percent loss in body weight in humans can cause sickness; a 20 percent loss means death. Water loss can happen quickly in a desert; 1 to 2 quarts of water loss per hour in a human can be fatal. To survive these conditions, hot-and-dry desert animals are often active only at night. They may burrow into the ground to escape the heat during the day. Some animals' fatty tissues can store water, such as a camel's hump or a Gila monster's tail. Other animals, such as a jackrabbit, get rid of body heat with long legs and ears that give off heat. The antelope squirrel can tolerate body temperatures above 104°F (40°C). Kangaroo rats and pocket mice get

Almost like Mars!

Studying both the Atacama and the extremely dry, cold parts of Antarctica called the Dry Valleys, scientists can go a long way toward understanding the limits of life and whether life could be possible on Mars. But the Atacama is not as dry and not nearly as cold as Mars. The Dry Valleys are very cold and nearly as dry as the Atacama. The Dry Valleys have not seen rainfall in recorded history. Except for a few steep rocks, they are the only parts of Antarctica without any ice. The Dry Valleys in Antarctica are mostly dead, because there are not enough hours of warmer temperatures for life to survive. But if scientists can find life in the Dry Valleys, then perhaps life could survive in similar conditions on Mars.

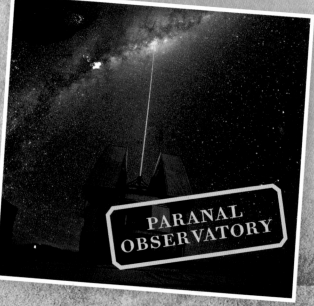

PARANAL OBSERVATORY

enough water just from eating seeds and grain.

You might think that no one would live in the Atacama, but there is a good reason for astronomers and scientists to love the place. The air is so dry that there are few clouds, and the air is very clear. It's the perfect place to observe the starry night skies. The Atacama is home to a number of observatories, including the Paranal Observatory and its Very Large Telescope (VLT) array. It's one of the world's most advanced optical telescopes. It can see stars four billion times fainter than a human eye can see.

The Snowiest and Iciest Places on Earth

The Paradise area on the south slope of Mount Rainier in Washington state is the snowiest place on Earth where snowfall is measured regularly. The average snowfall is 56 feet (17 meters) per year. That's about the height of a dozen children standing on each other's shoulders.

During the winter of 1971–1972, 93.5 feet (28.5 meters) of snow fell, setting a world record for that year! Snow can fall any day of the year in Paradise, even during the summer. More than 1 foot (30 centimeters) of snow fell during the summer of 1973. But the most snow in one year, 95 feet (29 meters), fell on the downhill ski area at Mount Baker, Washington, from July 1998 to June 1999. The most snow in any 24-hour period was more than 6 feet (1.8 meters) of snow, which fell at Silver Lake, Colorado. Silver Lake is nearly 2 miles (3.2 kilometers) above sea level, and lies just northwest of Denver. The record-breaking snowstorm began in the afternoon of April 14, 1921. It snowed and snowed and snowed. The blizzard continued nonstop for 32 hours. In those days, many homes in the area were heated by fireplaces or wood-burning stoves, and water was drawn from wells, so electric lines going down were not a problem for the residents. All this snow made for great skiing, but blizzards can be dangerous, too; avalanches are more likely after a big snowstorm.

Ancient ice tubes

Even though it doesn't snow very much in Antarctica, that continent still has the deepest ice on Earth. The ice covering Antarctica contains more than 90 percent of Earth's ice. Some of the ice sheets are more than 2.5 miles (4 kilometers) deep. If this ice were to melt, sea levels around the world could rise hundreds of feet or meters. In 2011, scientists in Antarctica drilled and extracted a 10,928-foot (3,331-meter) column of ice. Scientists hypothesize that some of the ice may be more than 100,000 years old, which they hope will offer clues to important questions about climate changes in the past. The study of ice cores helps scientists predict how the climate may change today and in the future.

Heavy snows on a mountaintop might slide down in a bunch of loose snow, creating a small avalanche called a sluff. That is not very dangerous. But a snow avalanche is a unit of snow, often times called a slab, that shatters down the side of a mountain. Natural avalanches happen because new or windblown snow overloads lower layers of snow or because of rapid warming. An average-size slab avalanche roars downhill at 60 to 80 miles (96 to 129 kilometers) per hour and reaches these speeds five seconds after it begins to move. It's like a runaway snow locomotive.

Deep snow will begin to slide if additional heavy snowfalls happen quickly. Several feet of snow added over several weeks is not a problem. But several feet of snow added in a snowstorm in a day or two is more dangerous. And several feet that piles up in a few hours because of strong winds is much more dangerous. Wind can deposit snow ten times faster than snow falls in a storm. Wind blows snow from the windy side of boulders and trees, and leaves snow on the downwind (lee) side. If the added weight of the new snow is added faster than the buried, weaker layer of snow can adjust to the load, the lower layer fractures and forms an avalanche.

Even worse, the weight of a person skiing or walking over the snow can trigger an avalanche in one-tenth of a second. That is why in the majority of avalanche accidents, the avalanche is triggered by the victim. People trapped in snow can't dig their way out; they must be dug out by a rescue party. Most people who are rescued within the first fifteen minutes survive. Many people owe their lives to having an avalanche beacon with them on the slopes. An avalanche beacon is a special radio that transmits a pulsed radio signal to help rescuers locate someone under snow. It's an important tool that may reduce the amount of time a person is buried.

Rain or snow, it's all water.

On average, 10 inches (25 centimeters) of snow is about equal to 1 inch (2.5 centimeters) of rain. Heavy, wet snow contains more water than dry, powdery snow. Snowmelt and spring runoff makes swollen rivers and streams run deep and fast. Melting snow can cause flooding and make for dangerous conditions for people who live near these waters.

The Highest Waterfall and the Steepest Drop on Earth

Imagine squirting a water pistol off the Empire State Building and then watching the stream of water fall to the ground. That waterfall would be small, only about one-third the height of Angel Falls in Venezuela, Earth's highest waterfall.

Waterfalls are rivers or streams flowing over a cliff or slope for a long enough distance to splash down into the water beneath. At Angel Falls, streams of water constantly pour from a height of 3,212 feet (979 meters) to the rapids below. The longest drop is 2,648 feet (807 meters), more than half a mile; then the water falls farther downhill in a series of cascades. Angel Falls is a plunge waterfall. That means that as the water flows over the cliff face it loses contact with the underlying rocks and boulders and plunges freely into space. Angel Falls is named after an American pilot, Jimmie Angel, who first saw the falls in the 1930s while looking for gold but accidentally crashed into them! Fortunately he and all his passengers escaped. The waterfall is so high that on some cloudy days people at the bottom can't see the top, and it seems as if the waterfall is coming straight out of the clouds. The water just below a waterfall is deep and is called a plunge pool. On the long trip down, much of the water sprays off as mist.

The state of Hawaii has three of the tallest waterfalls on Earth. Waihilau Falls, on the island of Hawaii, has a drop of 2,600 feet (792 meters), more than twice the height of the Empire State Building. The area around Waihilau Falls is very difficult to get to and looks much the same as it did in the past. The waterfall appears as a very tall and thin thread of white water falling down a steep cliff covered in lush greenery. The area has four very tall waterfalls, each more than 1,000 feet (305 meters) in height.

The steepest sheer drop on Earth is Mount Thor on Baffin Island in the Canadian Arctic. It is thought to be the highest purely vertical fall, at 4,100 feet (1,250 meters). The steep face of Mount Thor makes it popular with rock climbers. The average grade (angle) is 105 degrees, so the rocky face slightly overhangs climbers for most of their climb. Because there is no simple walk to the top, climbers use special climbing shoes, body harnesses, ropes, and anchors attached to the rocks to go up and come down safely. But even that scary, long fall is small compared to the highest drop in the

Look out belooowww!

One of the world's most famous water-falls is Niagara Falls, on the United States and Canadian border. More than 6 million cubic feet (1 million cubic meters) of water goes over Niagara Falls every minute. Each cubic foot (.03 cubic meter) of water weighs approximately 62 pounds (28 kilograms). That is the weight of about 200,000 elephants going over Niagara Falls every minute! Falling over the edge of a tall waterfall is dangerous. If the impact of hitting the water below from a great height didn't knock you out, the powerful, swirling currents in the plunge pool could cause you to drown. Nevertheless, some people have gone over Niagara Falls in barrels, and one person tried it on a Jet Ski (he didn't survive). Amazingly, most people who survived the fall over Niagara Falls went in wooden barrels. Several people just jumped. If a person were to survive, they would be arrested and fined.

solar system. This drop is called Verona Rupes, and it's on Miranda, a moon of Uranus. Verona Rupes is approximately a 12-mile (20-kilometer) drop straight down from a high cliff on Miranda. Now *that* cliff is worth shooting a water pistol from the top and watching the water drops fall!

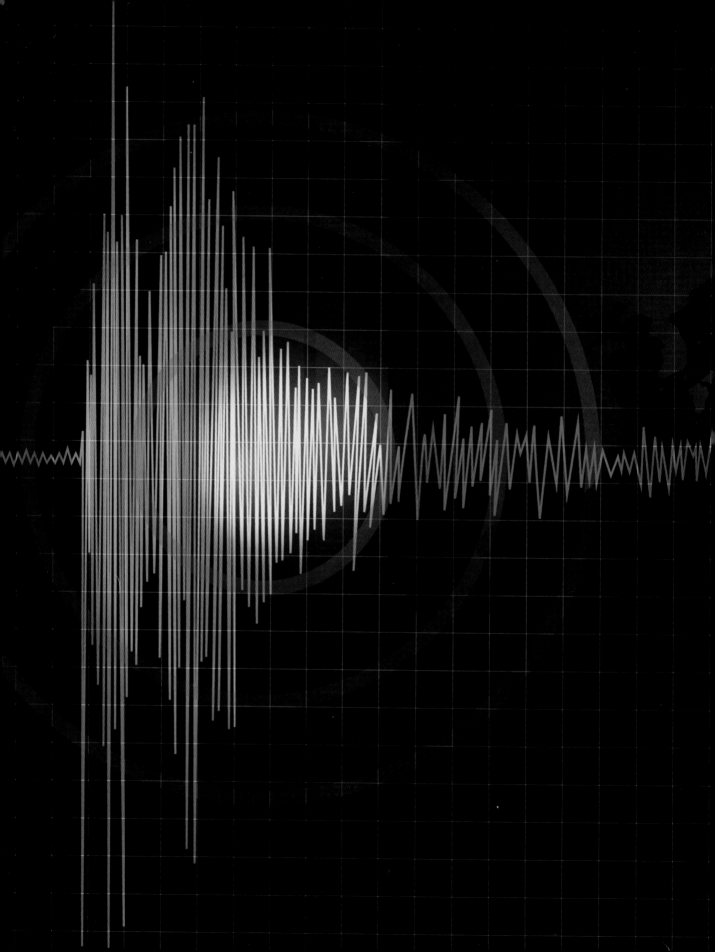

The Biggest Earthquake on Earth

Being in a large earthquake is like being on a scary ride in an amusement park—only you don't know when the ride is going to end. The ground shakes and rocks beneath your feet. Glass windows break, and walls in a house buckle under your hand and feel like rubber.

Standing water in a pool or an aquarium tank sloshes back and forth. Car alarms are triggered and the sirens add to the confusion. The rocking feels as if the quake lasts for a long time, though it may be only a minute or two. But even ten or twenty seconds in an earthquake feels like an eternity.

The May 22, 1960, earthquake in Valdivia, Chile, was the most powerful earthquake of the twentieth century. It measured 9.5 on the moment magnitude scale. It caused massive destruction, deaths, and injuries, and left more than two million people homeless. The giant quake was preceded by four quakes bigger than magnitude 7.0 and was followed by several aftershocks, with five that were magnitude 7.0 or greater. The earthquake triggered many landslides in valleys in the southern Andes Mountains. Two days after the earthquake, at least one nearby volcano erupted, sending ashes and steam thousands of feet into the air.

The states of Alaska and California, in North America, are the homes of the greatest number of earthquakes every year. The largest earthquake in North America was the March 1964 Alaskan quake. The shock was estimated to be three minutes long. Anchorage, 75 miles (120 kilometers) from the epicenter, suffered the most damage. In the downtown area, thirty blocks of buildings were destroyed.

The San Andreas Fault zone is where most earthquakes occur in California. The fault, a fracture or break in Earth's crust, is continuously moving and shifting. During the past three million years, the average rate of motion has been approximately 2 inches (5 centimeters) per year. That is about the same rate at which your fingernails grow. If that rate and direction continues, scientists say that Los Angeles and San Francisco will be next-door neighbors in fifteen million years—give or take a few thousand years.

Each year, Southern California has about ten thousand earthquakes. Most are too small to be noticeable, but several hundred are strong enough to be felt each year. Approximately fifteen to twenty of these quakes are greater than 4.0 in magnitude and cause damage.

A large earthquake will cause many aftershocks ranging from small to large for several months afterward. The magnitude of a quake is the same no matter where you are. The intensity of a quake is a measure of the shaking and varies depending on your location. The March 11, 2011, Japanese undersea earthquake off the Pacific coast of Tohoku was of the magnitude 9.0. It was the most powerful recorded earthquake ever to hit Japan and one of the five most powerful earthquakes recorded since 1900. It caused massive destruction on its own and triggered a huge tsunami that caused even worse destruction. The tsunami flooded hundreds of thousands of people out of their homes. It also caused a number of nuclear accidents and the meltdown of several reactors at the Fukushima nuclear power plant. Residents within a 12½-mile (20-kilometer) radius were evacuated from their homes.

How do you measure shake, rattle, and roll?

A seismometer is an instrument that measures and records the strength of earthquakes. The first seismometers were spring-pendulum devices. In these seismometers, a weight is attached to the frame by a spring or a pendulum. When an earthquake strikes, the relative motion between the weight and the frame is recorded on a chart called a seismogram. The first one ever built was developed in 1751. It wasn't for another hundred years that faults were recognized as the source of earthquakes. The largest spring-pendulum seismometer weighed approximately 15 tons (13,600 kilograms). There is a spring-pendulum still in use in Mexico City; it is approximately three stories tall. Today, most scientists use much smaller electronic seismometers, which use computers, to record earthquakes.

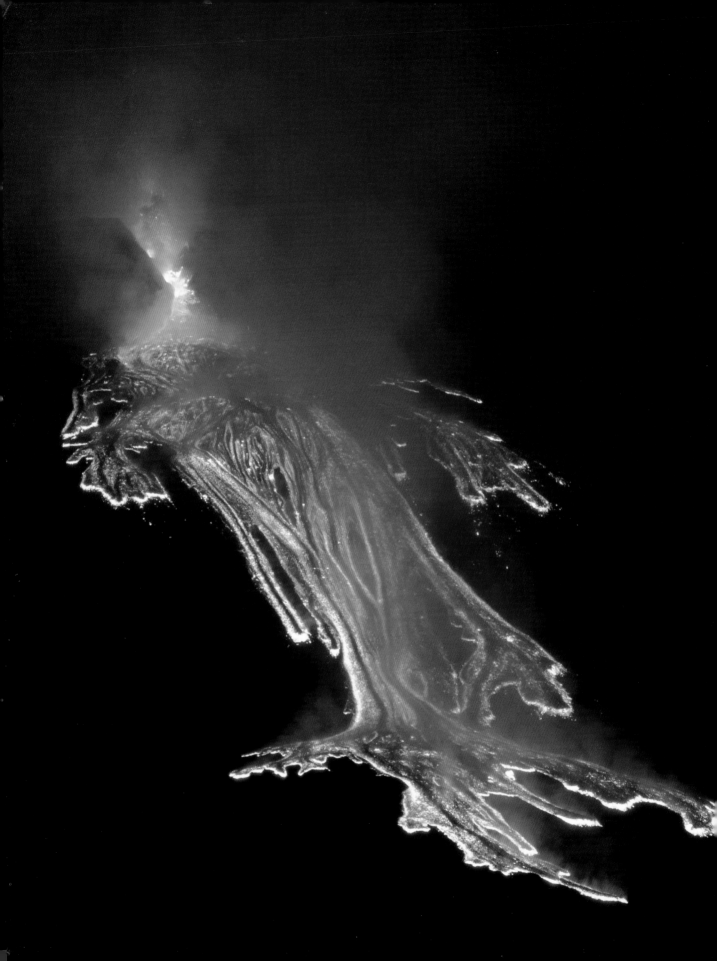

The Largest Volcanic Eruption on Earth

As you read this book, somewhere around the world there are approximately twenty volcanoes erupting. Three-quarters of volcanic eruptions occur unseen beneath the oceans, and no one knows when they happen.

Scientists use a scale called the Volcanic Explosivity Index (VEI) to measure the strength of volcanic blasts. The VEI runs from 1 to 8, with 8 being the biggest. A magnitude 8 eruption would blast out more than 240 cubic miles (1,000 cubic kilometers) of ash and rock into the atmosphere. It would be like watching a firework explode—only a volcanic eruption is millions of times bigger than the biggest firework you've ever seen.

The biggest eruptions are called super-eruptions. Scientists think that the largest one on Earth was at Lake Toba in Sumatra, Indonesia, approximately 73,000 years ago. The explosion released so much dust and rock into the air that it blocked sunlight for six to ten years and resulted in a volcanic winter and a worldwide ice age that lasted for 1,000 years. The largest volcanic eruption in modern times was Mount Tambora, Indonesia, on April 10, 1815. It is rated a 7 on the VEI. The eruption cast a cloud of ash around the world that lingered for several years. The sound of the explosion was heard 1,240 miles (2,000 kilometers) away. The ash blown into the air by the volcano blocked sunlight and lowered temperatures around the world by more than 5°F (3°C). The result was a strange year known as the "Year Without a Summer," in 1816. A foot (30 centimeters) of snow fell in Quebec in June. Crops failed worldwide because of the lack of sunlight. This caused one of the worst famines of the nineteenth century. More than 70,000 people died as a result.

Imagine a cloud of smoke and ash so thick that it could stop air traffic between Europe and the rest of the world for a week. That's what happened when a volcano erupted beneath glacial

An overnight sensation

Some volcanoes take thousands of years to form. Others can grow almost overnight. The volcano Parícutin appeared on February 20, 1943, in a Mexican cornfield. Within a week it was five stories tall, and by the end of a year it was 1,102 feet (336 meters) high.

ice in Iceland in the spring of 2010. The cold water from the melting ice chilled the lava quickly and broke it into small pieces of rock and ash. The ash poured upward, high into the atmosphere, and was carried by winds over the busy airplane lanes of Europe. More than 95,000 flights were canceled and millions of people were stranded in Europe and around the world.

PARICUTIN

What is lava?

The molten rock within Earth is called magma. Molten rock that flows out of a volcano is called lava. Fresh lava ranges from 1,300°F to 2,200°F (700°C to 1,200°C) and glows red hot to white hot as it flows. That is seven to ten times as hot as boiling water. Lava can erupt by slowly bubbling out of a volcano or by spurting out in explosions or lava fountains. When lava cools it forms many different shapes and types of rock. The two main types have Hawaiian names. *Pahoehoe* is a smooth, dark lava rock and can form flat areas that sometimes look like parking lots. *A'a* forms jagged rocks from a few inches (centimeters) to many feet (meters) in size. *Pahoehoe* is easy to walk on, while *a'a* is difficult to walk across.

The Most Destructive Tsunami on Earth

On December 26, 2004, an earthquake released the energy of 23,000 atomic bombs under the Indian Ocean. The 9.1 to 9.3 magnitude earthquake was the third largest earthquake ever recorded.

It lasted approximately ten minutes, the longest time ever observed for a quake. Ten minutes of the ground shaking in an earthquake can feel like a scary roller-coaster ride that lasts for ten hours. It caused all of planet Earth to vibrate like a struck gong. It also triggered other earthquakes around the world, some as far away as Alaska.

The gigantic quake unleashed a series of killer tsunami waves that traveled 600 miles (965 kilometers) per hour, as fast as a jetliner, across the Indian Ocean. The total energy of the tsunami waves is estimated to be more than the combined explosive energy of World War II. The giant waves, some 100 feet (32 meters) high, flooded coastal areas in Indonesia, Sri Lanka, India, and Thailand. The tsunami traveled as far as 3,000 miles (4,828 kilometers) to the coast of Africa. Nearly 230,000 people were killed in fourteen different countries.

Tsunamis behave very differently in deep ocean water than in shallow water near a coastline. In deep water, tsunami waves form only a small bulge, barely noticeable and harmless, but traveling at jet-plane speed of 300 to 600 miles (483 to 966 kilometers) per hour. These kinds of tsunamis travel across the ocean in a series of small waves each only a few feet (meters) high, with each wave crest as far as 60 miles (96 kilometers) apart from the next wave crest. The waves can cross thousands of miles of ocean water without losing much energy. In shallow water near coastlines, tsunamis slow down to only a few miles (kilometers) per hour, but form large, destructive waves that grow in height and have the force to lift and flip ships, demolish docks, and destroy houses thousands of feet inland.

Despite several hours between the 2004 Indian Ocean earthquake and the distant impact of the tsunami waves on land, nearly all of the victims were taken by surprise. There were no tsunami early-warning systems in place in the Indian Ocean. Tsunamis are much more frequent in the Pacific Ocean because of the Ring of Fire, an area circling the Pacific where earthquakes and volcanoes often occur. The Pacific has long had a tsunami early-warning system in place.

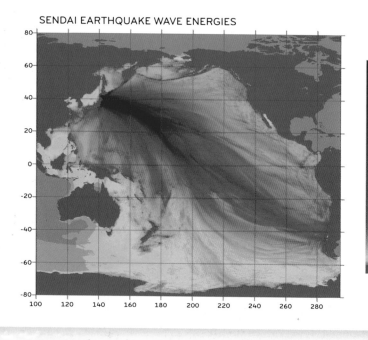

SENDAI EARTHQUAKE WAVE ENERGIES

120 [cm]
110 [cm]
100 [cm]
90 [cm]
80 [cm]
70 [cm]
60 [cm]
50 [cm]
40 [cm]
30 [cm]
20 [cm]
10 [cm]
0 [cm]

TSUNAMI EVACUATION ROUTE

One of the largest tsunamis ever was set off by the Great East Japan Earthquake of March 11, 2011. The 9.0 earthquake caused a tsunami that destroyed much of the Pacific coast of Japan's northern islands, devastated an entire town, and caused the loss of thousands of lives. The tsunami waves went over walls and caught people in buildings on higher ground, who thought they were safe. It washed away bridges and overtopped walls that had been thought to protect against any tsunami waves. On the slope of a mountain near the coastline, scientists found wave destruction up to 127 feet (39 meters) high. The damage from the tsunami was even worse than the damage from the original earthquake.

The seventh wave.

Hawaii gets about one tsunami a year and a damaging "big one" approximately every seven years. On April 1, 1946, the coast of Hilo Island was hit by 30-foot (9-meter) waves shattering onto land at 500 miles (805 kilometers) per hour.

Index

Photo Credits

Permission to use the following photographs is gratefully acknowledged:

Seymour Simon has been called "the dean of the [children's science book] field" by the *New York Times*. He has written more than 250 books for young readers and has received the American Association for the Advancement of Science/ Subaru Lifetime Achievement Award for his lasting contribution to children's science literature, the Science Books & Films Key Award for Excellence in Science Books, the Empire State Award for excellence in literature for young people, and the Educational Paperback Association Jeremiah Ludington Award. He and his wife, Liz Nealon, live in Great Neck, New York. You can visit him online at his Webby Award Honoree website, www.seymoursimon.com, where you can also download a free, four-page teacher guide to accompany this book.

Also by Seymour Simon

Praise for *Seymour Simon's Extreme Oceans*:

"Will appeal particularly to young scientists who are interested in nature and animals as well as to those who are pulled in by dangerous scenarios and esoteric facts."
 —*School Library Journal*

"A solid addition to science collections."
 —*Booklist*

"Should spark readers' interest in marine life."
 —*Publishers Weekly*

NSTA-CBC Outstanding Science Trade Book